AF230961

Whether you are a child or an adult, you can sometimes feel lost, hoping that you will find someone who can help.

Perhaps that someone will give you a map or point you in the right direction.

This book is to help you find your own direction by understanding yourself better.

How does that sound to you?

What are you missing?
'Open up your senses'

Part of the NLP for Everyone Series

by
Monika Clough

Acknowledgements

A huge thank you to those listed below for making this book possible.
'Yippee we've made it'.
~ My husband Roger, for his ongoing support and technology meddling ~
~ Chris and Glenda Grimsley, NLP in the Northwest ~
~ Tim Perkins, Wizards Keep Ltd for writing the foreword for the second edition ~
~ Sarah and Mabel ~
~ Carl and Josh ~
~ Abigail and her Brownies ~

Foreword

I first met Monika, when she was a student of mine on my *Fantasy Art Unlimited* course, a few years ago. She was enthusiastic about creating and I saw a spark in her, which would help her to achieve her goals a few years later.

Her passion and enthusiasm has continued to grow over time and this, added to her natural humble charm, has meant that, as I expected, she broke the mould; unlike many of her contemporaries and she made the move to create her own book.

This is no mean feat and I speak from the experience of having worked for Marvel and DC as a comic creator as well as a great many other publishers, and in film and TV too. Nowadays, I work on my own books and I realise the immense effort it takes to get a book from concept to print. It takes a lot of grit and determination to achieve this goal and not many people ever get past the initial stages.

Many obstacles stand in the way of anyone wanting to have a book published; life itself can prove incredibly difficult at times, then there is the actual concept itself, followed by the realisation of the content, deadlines, sourcing print, pre-press proofing, going to print, marketing, selling, etc. And that is just for starters.

To do this and have a pedigree of publications for the top publishers in the world is hard enough to achieve, but to do this without any previous work to show is certainly no mean feat and I have to take my hat off here and say, 'Well done, Monika, I am so proud of you!' I cannot commend her spirit enough.

Now, all that said and done, sheer determination and tenacity are simply not enough – without having the right quality of content.

Her lovely illustrated book, 'What are you missing?', is testament to her ability to follow through on her dream; now a reality. It's a great informative read, with a lovely story for kids that is richly illustrated in Monika's own unique style, which I have been lucky enough to see her develop.

I won't spoil the content of the story of the book by describing what you are about to read, but I will say you are in for a treat. I can tell you it contains information about Neuro-linguistic programming (NLP). Wow doesn't that sound grand? NLP divides people's learning styles into three major categories which are auditory, visual and kinaesthetic – so you will learn all this and more, and have a better understanding of how all of us learn differently and so should be taught accordingly.

This is a book for everyone. For small children – it's a cute, illustrated bedtime story. For older children – it's a great way to learn about NLP and for the adults it can be used like a manual to help understand each other's needs better.

All that remains now, is for you to settle down and have a fun read, I did.

Tim Perkins
Wizards Keep
March 2019

Introduction

For the adults

In the world of technology we now live in, we know almost everything about computers and mobile phones. Yet there is one computer we don't seem to know a lot about – our own computer; our *brain*. It doesn't come with a manual and there aren't really any courses teaching us how to operate it. When you are a guardian, a parent or a teacher, not only are you trying to figure out your own brain but you are also helping the young ones to understand theirs – not an easy task. I hope this book will be a good starting point.

Here's how the book works:

• for little ones, there is an illustrated story inside; ideal for bedtime

• older children will be able to learn more about NLP and can go on to do their own research

• adults may use this book as a manual. There are plenty of exercises you can do with the young ones. It is a fun way to understand each other better

I very much look forward to receiving your feedback and suggestions. Remember, we are all on this amazing journey of discovery and when we join forces together, we can make this journey *fantastic*!

For the children

This book is to help you feel *fantastic* by understanding yourself better. You will set out on an adventure, exploring your feelings and those of people around you. After each step you take you will notice that you start to feel happier, get along better with your family, friends and any other people you might meet.

I hope you are excited.

Neuro-linguistic programming

There are lots of ways to learn about yourself and I encourage you to have a go at as many as you can. The one that I found the most helpful and easy to explain is called Neuro-linguistic programming (NLP). It sounds complicated but what does NLP mean? Let's break it down:

Neuro – explains how the mind and body work together. For example, you are playing outside on a sunny day, only wearing shorts and a T-shirt. Later on, the sun becomes covered by clouds, it's getting windy and starts raining. You begin to feel cold, your mind then sends a message to your body. As a result, you get goosebumps, you start to shiver, your skin becomes pale and, if you don't get warmer soon, your lips and nails may turn blue.

Linguistic – or simply 'language'. It teaches us how to understand what is going on in people's heads by observing their language. Here we are playing detectives looking for 3 main clues:

- what words they use
- what the tone of their voice is
- what body language they use

Let's get back to our situation where you are outside in the rain feeling cold. What words would you use? You probably say something like 'I feel cold, I am freezing, my legs are shivering.' What would be the tone of your voice? You could be shouting, crying or your voice could be trembling through cold. What would your body language be like? You might curl up in a ball to protect yourself, you might rub your hands against your arms and legs to warm up or you could also be jumping on the spot.

Programming – it shows us how we behave; what do we do in any particular situation. Using our previous example, how would you behave? You could shout and wait for somebody to help you, you could run home and have a warm bath or you could find a dry shelter and wait until the rain passes.

Why did I create this book?

All of my life, and I am now quite grown-up, I wanted to understand people, what makes them happy or sad. How can I talk to lots of people without upsetting anybody? What do I need to do to find great friends and keep them?

Going back to the definition of NLP, when you know, what's happening in your mind, what language you use and how you behave (your program) you then have the power to change what you want to change and keep what you want to keep. NLP is helping me to achieve that and I hope it can help you too.

Are you ready?

Each day from the moment we wake up there is a whole world of experiences just waiting for us. There is a lot going on around us and although our mind is very powerful, we cannot pay full attention to everything all the time. We make choices about what we concentrate on and what we ignore. That is all OK as long as we remember that it was us who made the choice and that someone else might have made a different choice; that is also OK.

Imagine the world being a giant supermarket. You enter knowing that you can buy everything there. You get your trolley and begin to shop. Have you ever noticed that there are some aisles you can spend hours looking around and some aisles you just pass without looking at anything? It doesn't mean that the items in that aisle are bad, you are just not interested in them because you made a choice. After spending some time in your favourite aisle you then pick some favourite things, put them in your trolley and take them home with you. You have made another choice.

This is what we do every single day.
We make choices!

Exercise

1. What choices do you make? Have a little chat with your friends.

2. Do you think choices depend on a person's age?

3. Next time you go to the supermarket with grown-ups, pay attention to what they are buying.

   What choices do they make?
   Make some notes in the box below.

When I was a child, I spent a lot of time reading; fairy tales, adventures and historical novels.

I learnt all about the choices the characters had to make, what they were missing and the consequences of both. I'm hoping that my little tale will do the same for you.

There is an old saying 'A picture is worth a thousand words' and this is why this story is full of illustrations to help you understand better.

Now make yourself
comfortable and
enter the wonderful land
of

fantasy

and

imagination.

It was another beautiful morning in Prickly Woods.
Daddy Mushroom was already working in the garden and Mummy Mushroom was in the kitchen.
Jacob Mushroom was in the kitchen with his mummy.

He was sat by the window just staring out.
He was so bored!

'Are you going outside to play with your friends Jacob? It's a lovely day,' said Mummy Mushroom. She was busy decorating a cake but could see that her son looked unhappy.

'They always play the same game. It's boring. I'd rather stay at home.'

'Well perhaps you could help me and take this cake to Mrs Fox; it's her favourite flavour.'

'OK. If I have to,' said Jacob, in a very dreary voice.

Mrs Fox lived in the darkest part of Prickly Woods. It was a *very* long walk and it took Jacob almost an hour.

Finally, through the trees, he could see the chimney of Mrs Fox's tree cottage.

'What a lovely surprise!' Said Mrs Fox. 'Your
Mum makes the most wonderful cakes. It runs
in your family you know. Your great-grandfather
was a famous baker.'

'Now let me look at you. Oh my, haven't
you grown! It's been a while since you
came to visit but I expect you're probably
busy spending time with your friends.'

Jacob said sulkily. 'Not exactly.
The truth is, I find them boring;
everything they do is boring.'

'I can see you need cheering up.
How about going on a trip?' Asked Mrs Fox.

'I suppose we could since I have nothing
better to do. Where are we going?' Asked
Jacob.

Mrs Fox looked towards her bookshelves and after a little bit of rummaging, she brought a large white paper painted with lines, squares and other shapes.

She studied it for a minute or two, then placed her finger right in the middle and said 'Here, this is where we are going. Jacob you will be in charge of this white paper which is called a *map*. It will help us to find the place.'

Mrs Fox grabbed her special sparkle and off they went.

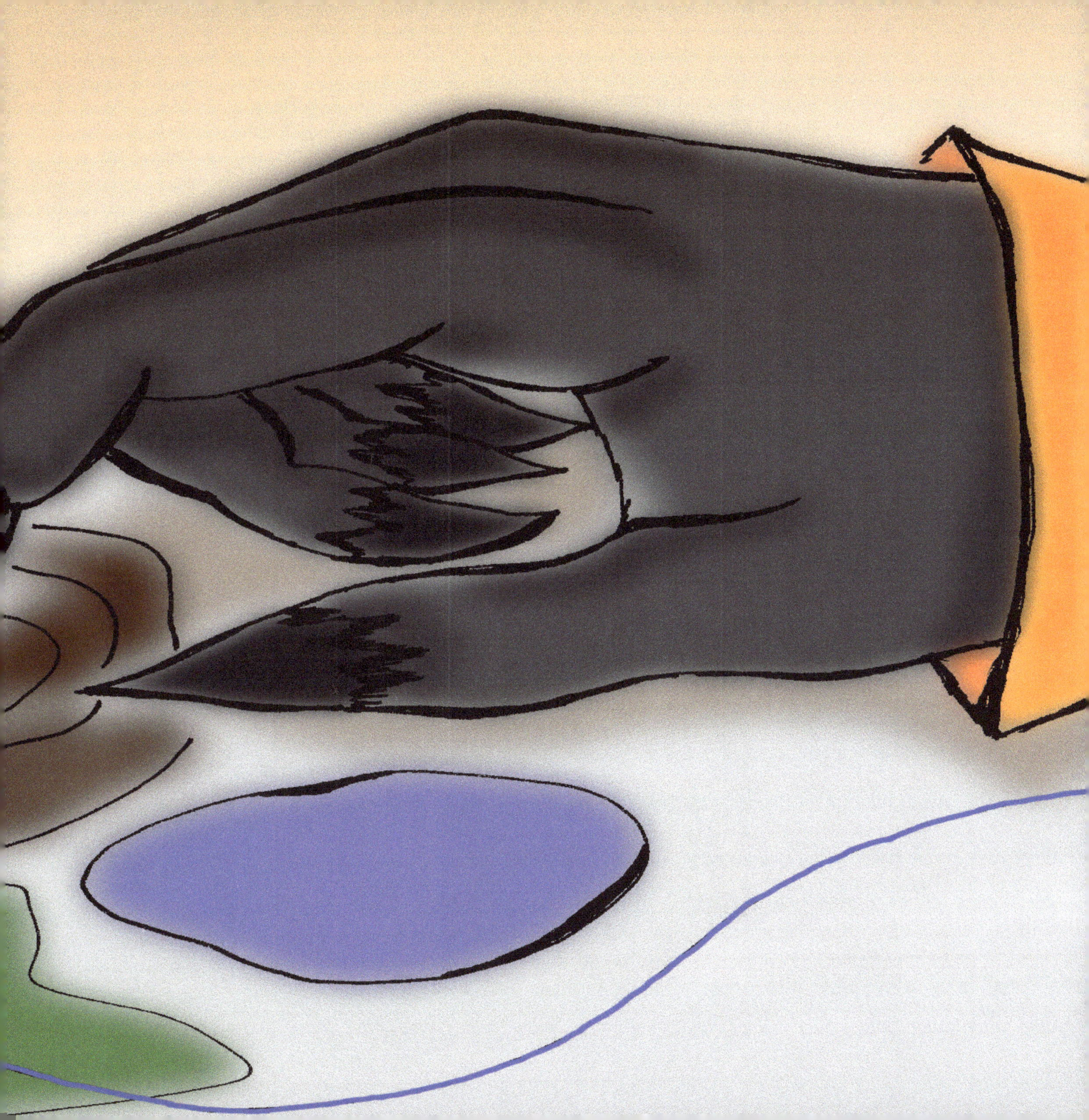

Their little walk seemed to take forever, at least in Jacob's mind. He became tired and had to rest under the tree a couple of times but was too curious to give up.

That thing called a *map* seemed really fascinating. Jacob could not take his eyes off it.

'We are here; isn't it a beautiful place!' Said Mrs Fox.
Jacob was still busy staring at the map didn't look at all impressed.
'Perhaps when you lift your head and start paying attention, you might feel differently,' replied Mrs Fox.

What a beautiful place!
Look how blue the sky is.
Can you hear the birds singing?
Mmm, I can smell the berries.
Shall we taste some?

Jacob dropped the map and looked around. There were mountains, trees and blue skies.
'So you're telling me, that all those colourful lines, squares and circles in the map look like this in real life. That is the coolest thing I've ever seen. It's like a secret code so nobody could find this place.'

'And that's not all,' said Mrs Fox and she took Jacob to the river.

It was beautiful with lots of berry bushes.

They drank fresh water from the river and munched on some berries.

They rested on the soft grass, enjoyed the warm sun and listened to the bird's song.

On the gentle breeze was the wonderful smell of the pine trees.

There was so much to experience.

'It's time to go before your Mum gets worried,' said Mrs Fox. 'Take this map with you to remind you of today's lesson.'

'What do you mean by lesson, Mrs Fox?'

'Well look at this map. It uses symbols to tell you what is there and which way to go but it cannot describe the real world. It doesn't tell you what sounds you can hear, what colours the flowers are and how they smell. You have to learn to open up all your senses; *sight*, *smell*, *touch*, *taste* and *hearing* to fully enjoy everything. Earlier on you mentioned your friends. You said that they're playing the same boring game but what else is there. Are they happy? Do they talk, laugh or sing when they're playing? What are you missing, Jacob? Think about it and remember to open up your senses. I hope I'll see you soon.'

'You will Mrs Fox and thank you for today.' Jacob waved goodbye and left for home.

'Mum, Mum. I had the most amazing day!' Jacob ran into the house shouting.

'I knew you would.' Said Mummy Mushroom.

'But how could you've known that?" Asked Jacob.

'Because Mushroom Mums know everything and now it's time for bed. Off you go; goodnight Jacob.'

Now it's your turn...

...open up your senses.

Sight - eyes

Words and phrases related to *sight*.

look   picture   colourful   clear   bright

I *see* what you mean.

Imagine this beautiful house.

People with a sight preference are usually very neat. They speak fast and like to doodle during long talks or long boring lessons!

Exercise

1. Draw one of the following fruits in the box below: apple, banana, orange or pear.

2. Have a chat or think about what present you would buy for a friend who mainly uses their sight sense.

   Write it down in the box.

Hearing - ears

Words and phrases related to *hearing*.

quiet *click* *harmony* *voice* *sound*

It's *music* to my ears.

Let's *hear* your plan.

People with a hearing preference are usually very sensitive to noise, take words literally and will like comic books with word bubbles, as their brain treats the seen words as though they are being heard!

Exercise

1. Ask a friend to fill small containers with sand, coins, rice, or buttons without showing you what's in the jar.

2. Now close your eyes and let your friend shake the jar. Can you tell what is in the jar just by listening?

3. What type of activity do people with hearing preference like to do? Write them in the box below.

4. Can you think of any other words to describe the things we hear? Write those down too.

Taste - tongue

Words and phrases related to *taste*.

sour   flavour   delicious   bitter

He was a *sweet* boy.

We need to *spice* up this football match.

People with a taste preference will use taste related words in their language - it will probably be food related! They will also be able to pick out a taste out of a medley of flavours.

Exercise

1. For this you will need some sugar.

2. With some of your friends, each of you put some sugar on your tongue. Some put it on the tip of the tongue, the others put it on the back of the tongue.

3. See how it tastes to each of you – do you taste it differently? Write down those differences and where the sugar was put on the tongue.

4. Find out what the basic tastes are. What is your favourite? Write it down below.

Touch - skin

Words and phrases related to *touch*.

warm sensitive soft rough fluffy

They gave us a *warm* welcome.

This task was a *breeze* for him.

People with a touch preference will use their hands to look at something – feel it – feel the texture. They speak slowly, wear comfortable clothes and cannot sit still for very long.

Exercise

1. For this you will need some pine cones, dice, a feather, some coins etc.

2. With some of your friends, cover some of the objects with a towel.

3. See if you can all guess what the objects are by feeling them through the cloth.

4. Can you think of any other words and phrases related to touch? Write them down in the box.

Smell - nose

Words and phrases related to *smell*.

fresh aroma fishy smelly odour

Something *fishy* is going on.

I *smell* a rat.

People with a smell preference have a very keen sense of smell. They can pick up any scent and love to be surrounded by comforting aromas.

Exercise

1. Put mint, garlic, cinnamon, rose petals and coffee beans in different pots.

2. Can you:

   a) identify each one by its smell?

   b) name animals that rely on their sense of smell? Write them down in the box below.

   c) think of a job that you would need a good sense of smell for? Again, write it in the box.

Yippee!

You've gained more knowledge about the senses. The next step is to find out how can you use it.

Each person has a different sense preference, we sometimes call them filters. Some of us might even have more than one preferred filter. Knowing the person's preferred sense/filter makes the communication a lot easier. Let's look at Sarah's story.

Sarah has a strong sight preference. She wanted to invite Harry to watch a movie with her in the local cinema, so she sent him a text message Harry has a strong hearing preference, he likes to talk to people and very often ignores anything written. Sarah didn't get a reply, got angry and went to the cinema with Jane instead. The next day at school, Harry found out about Sarah's trip to the cinema and got upset for not being invited. Luckily, Sarah read this book about senses and decided to put it into practice. She phoned Harry, they had a long chat and organised another trip to the cinema.

On the way home, Sarah gave Harry this little book about senses. It was a perfect afternoon.

A month later Harry went to Sarah's birthday party. He bought her this gorgeous colourful bracelet as a gift. Harry learnt about Sarah's preferred sense and knew that this would make her smile.

Now, put it all into practice.

Exercise

1. So, how can you tell your friend's preferred sense/filter?
2. Listen for the words and phrases I've included for each sense;
3. Pay attention to their behaviour, how they dress, what subjects they like at school, what their hobbies are
4. How they learn new things. Do they:
   a) read the instructions (sight);
   b) listen to the instructions (hearing);
   c) follow the instructions (smell, taste, touch).
   Make some notes below.

Good luck on your journey!

9 781912 677085